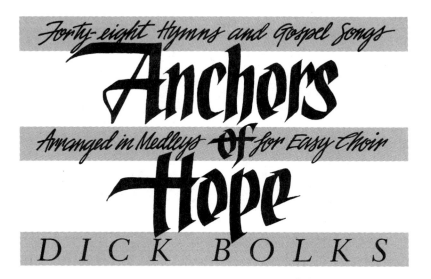

Forty-eight Hymns and Gospel Songs

Anchors

Arranged in Medleys **of** for Easy Choir

Hope

DICK BOLKS

See inside back cover for Table of Contents.

*L*illenas **PUBLISHING COMPANY**

KANSAS CITY, MO 64141

All Hail the Power Medley

All Hail the Power of Jesus' Name (Coronation and Diadem)
Blessed Be the Name

Arr. by Dick Bolks

"All Hail the Power of Jesus' Name" (Perronet - Ellor)

"Blessed Be the Name" (Clark - Hudson)

I Want to Be like Jesus Medley

I Want to Be Like Jesus
Have Thine Own Way, Lord

Arr. by Dick Bolks

*"I Want to Be Like Jesus" (Chisholm - Ives)

I have one deep, su - preme de - sire,

That I may be like Je - sus.

"Have Thine Own Way, Lord" (Pollard - Stebbins)

Wonderful Medley

It Is Truly Wonderful
This Is Like Heaven to Me

Arr. by Dick Bolks

"It Is Truly Wonderful" (Barney E. Warren)

1. He par - doned my trans - gres - sions; He
   not a sin - gle bless - ing Which

sanc - ti - fied my soul; He hon - ors my con -
we re - ceive on earth That does not come from

fes - sions Since by His blood I'm whole. It is
heav - en, The source of our new birth. It is

(13) tru - ly won-der-ful what the Lord has done! It is tru - ly won-der-ful! It is

tru - ly won-der-ful! It is tru - ly won-der-ful what the Lord has done!

2nd time: rit. 1. Glo - ry to His name!

2. There's name!

"This Is Like Heaven to Me" (J. E. French)

Men unison

Ladies unison

1. We

God's Love Within Medley

O Love That Will Not Let Me Go
Love Divine, All Loves Excelling
Spirit of God, Descend

Arr. by Dick Bolks

"Love Divine, All Loves Excelling" (Wesley - Zundel)

1st time: Men unison
2nd time: S.A.T.B.

Brighter ♩ = 92

1. Love di - vine, all loves ex - cell - ing, Joy of heav'n, to earth come down!
2. Fin - ish then Thy new cre - a - tion; Pure and spot - less let us be.

1st time: S.A.

Fix in us Thy hum - ble dwell - ing; All Thy faith - ful mer - cies crown.
Let us see Thy great sal - va - tion, Per - fect - ly re - stored in Thee.

Both times: S.A.T.B.

Je - sus, Thou art all com - pas - sion; Pure, un - bound - ed love Thou art.
Changed from glo - ry in - to glo - ry, Till in heav'n we take our place,

2nd time: rit.

Vis - it us with Thy sal - va - tion; En - ter ev - 'ry trem - bling heart.
Till we cast our crowns be - fore Thee, Lost in won - der,

love, and praise. Oo

"Spirit of God, Descend" (Croly - Atkinson)

Settled Medley

The Old Account Settled
I Would Not Be Denied
I Have Settled the Question

Arr. by Dick Bolks

"The Old Account Settled" (F. M. Graham)

1st time: Ladies unison
2nd time: Choir unison

1. There was a time on earth When in the book of heav'n, An old ac-count was stand-ing For sins yet un-for-giv'n; My name was at the top, And man-y things be-low. I went un-to the Keep-er, And set-tled long a-go. Long a-

2. When in that hap-py home, My Sav-ior's home a-bove, I'll sing re-demp-tion's sto-ry, And praise Him for His love; I'll not for-get that book, With pag-es white as snow, Be-cause I came and set-tled, And set-tled long a-go.

1st time: Men unison

S.A.T.B.

"I Would Not Be Denied" (C. P. Jones)

Peace Medley

Sweet Peace, the Gift of God's Love
Wonderful Peace
Thou Wilt Keep Him in Perfect Peace

Arr. by Dick Bolks

"Sweet Peace, the Gift of God's Love" (Peter P. Bilhorn)

There comes to my heart one sweet strain,_____ A glad and a joy-ous re-frain;_____ I

28

Tell the Story Medley

I Love to Tell the Story
We've a Story to Tell to the Nations
Tell the Blessed Story

Arr. by Dick Bolks

"We've a Story to Tell to the Nations" (W. Ernest Nichol)
With vigor ♩ = 100

1. We've a sto - ry to tell to the na - tions That shall
   mes - sage to give to the na - tions That the

turn their hearts to the right,_____ A sto - ry of truth and____
Lord who reign - eth a - bove_____ Hath sent us His Son to____

mer - cy, A sto - ry of peace and light,_____ A
save_____ us, And show us that God is love,_____ And

sto - ry of peace and light._____
show us that God is love._____ For the dark - ness shall turn to

1st time: S.A.T.B.
2nd time: Ladies unison

*"Tell the Blessed Story" (Haldor Lillenas)

Men unison

Church of God, a - wak - en; heed the Lord's com - mand. Tell the bless - ed

sto - ry of the Cross. Fields are white for har - vest - ing on

Ladies unison

ev - 'ry hand. Tell the bless-ed sto - ry of the Cross.

With conviction
S.A.T.B.

Tell the bless-ed sto - ry of the cross of Je - sus. Tell the bless-ed sto - ry of the

Till Jesus Comes Medley

Every Bridge Is Burned Behind Me
We'll Work Till Jesus Comes
I Feel Like Traveling On
When the Battle's Over

Arr. by Dick Bolks

"Every Bridge Is Burned Behind Me" (Oatman - Hugg)

Since I start-ed out to find Thee, Since I to the Cross did flee, Ev-'ry bridge is burned be-hind me; I will nev-er turn from Thee. Strength-en all the

In the Garden Medley

In the Garden
The Beautiful Garden of Prayer

Arr. by Dick Bolks

"In the Garden" (C. Austin Miles)

44

there,   None   oth-er   has   ev-er_____   known._____

rall.

*"The Beautiful Garden of Prayer" (Schroll - Fillmore)

Ladies unison *a tempo*

There's a   gar-den   where   Je-sus   is   wait-ing;_____

There's a   place   that   is   won-drous-ly   fair,_____

Men unison

_____   For   it   glows   with   the   light   of   His   pres-ence._____

Call to Praise Medley

Brethren, We Have Met to Worship
Come, Christians, Join to Sing
O Come, Let Us Adore Him

"Brethren, We Have Met to Worship" (Atkins - Moore)

Arr. by Dick Bolks

Prayerfully, freely

*If necessary, piano may be used. Trax enter at meas. 18.

*Begin tape track.

50

"O Come, Let Us Adore Him" (Traditional)

Love Medley

My Jesus, I Love Thee
More Love to Thee

Arr. by Dick Bolks

"My Jesus, I Love Thee" (Featherstone - Gordon)

"More Love to Thee" (Prentiss - Doane)
1st time: Men unison
2nd time: S.A.T.B.

1. More love to Thee, O Christ, More love to Thee!
2. Once earth - ly joy I craved, Sought peace and rest.

1st time: Ladies unison

Hear Thou the prayer I make On bend - ed
Now Thee a - lone I seek; Give what is

Atoning Blood Medley

Nothing but the Blood
Are You Washed in the Blood?
There Is Power in the Blood

Arr. by Dick Bolks

58

"Are You Washed in the Blood?" (Elisha A. Hoffmann)

Have you been to Je-sus for the cleans - ing pow'r? Are you washed in the blood of the Lamb? Are you ful - ly trust-ing in His grace this hour? Are you washed in the blood of the Lamb? Are you washed in the blood, In the soul - cleans-ing blood of the

Are you washed in the blood,

"There Is Power in the Blood" (Lewis E. Jones)

Anchor Medley

The Haven of Rest
My Anchor Holds
We Have an Anchor

Arr. by Dick Bolks

"The Haven of Rest" (Gilmour - Moore)

"My Anchor Holds" (Martin - Towner)

64

"We Have an Anchor" (Owens - Kirkpatrick)

Adoration Medley

I Know a Name
Jesus Is the Sweetest Name I Know
A Name I Highly Treasure

Arr. by Dick Bolks

*"I Know a Name" (Haldor Lillenas)

I know a name that can drive a-way all sor-row;

I know a name that is sweet-er than them all;

I know a name from which com-fort I may bor-row,

When oth-ers fail and when tears of an-guish fall.

I know a name, a won-der-ful

name; That won-der-ful name is

Jesus. There have been names that I have loved to

"Jesus Is the Sweetest Name I Know" (Lela Long)

hear, But nev-er has there been a name so dear

*"A Name I Highly Treasure" (Oscar C. Eliason)

Heaven Medley

We'll Understand It Better
The Eastern Gate
The Happy Jubilee

Arr. by Dick Bolks

"We'll Understand It Better"
(C. A. Tindley)

1st time: Ladies unison
2nd time: Men unison

1. We are of-ten tossed and driv'n on the rest-less sea of time, Som-ber
   dark on ev-'ry hand, and we can-not un-der-stand All the

Both times: Choir unison

skies and howl-ing tem-pests oft suc - ceed a bright sun-shine; In that land of per-fect day, when the
ways that God would lead us to that bless-ed Prom-ised land; But He'll guide us with His eye, and we'll

mists have rolled a-way, We will un-der-stand it bet-ter by and by.
fol-low till we die, For we'll un-der-stand it bet-ter by and by.

"The Eastern Gate" (I. G. Martin)

*"The Happy Jubilee" (Browning - Pace)

Lord, I've been in-vit-ed to a meet-ing in the air, Ju-bi-lee,___ Ju-bi-lee, Ju-bi-lee!___ Ju-bi-lee! All the saints of all the a-ges in their glo-ry will be there; Oh, I'm go-ing to that hap-py ju-bi-lee, ju-bi-lee! Ju-bi-lee! ju-bi-lee!

Drawing Nearer Medley

I Am Thine, O Lord
Nearer, My God, to Thee
Close to Thee

Arr. by Dick Bolks

"I Am Thine, O Lord" (Crosby - Doane)

1. I am Thine, O Lord; I have
crate me now to Thy

heard Thy voice, And it told Thy love to____ me. But I
ser - vice, Lord, By the pow'r of grace di - vine. Let my

long to rise in the arms of faith, And be clos - er drawn to
soul look up with a stead - fast hope, And my will be lost in

"Nearer, My God, to Thee" (Adams - Mason)

"Close to Thee" (Crosby - Vail)

Infilling Medley

Come, Every One That Is Thirsty
Bring Your Vessels, Not a Few

Arr. by Dick Bolks

"Bring Your Vessels, Not a Few" (Lelia N. Morris)

1st time: Ladies unison
2nd time: Men unison

1. Are you long-ing for the full-ness of the bless-ing of the
   cruse of oil un-fail-ing is His grace for-ev-er-

Lord in your heart and life to - day? Claim the prom-ise of your Fa-ther; come ac-
more, And His love un-chang-ing still; And ac-cord-ing to His prom-ise, with the

cord-ing to His Word, In the bless - ed old - time way. He will
Ho - ly Ghost and pow'r He will ev - 'ry ves - sel fill.

Guidance Medley

O God, Our Help in Ages Past
Guide Me, O Thou Great Jehovah

Arr. by Dick Bolks

"O God, Our Help in Ages Past" (Watts - Croft)

O God, our help in a - ges past, Our

hope for years to come, Our shel - ter from the

storm - y blast, And our e - ter - nal home! Un -

"Guide Me, O Thou Great Jehovah" (Williams - Hughes)